What the Words Whisper

Alaina Kubiak

BookLeaf Publishing

Presentation by *BookLeaf Publishing*

Web: www.bookleafpub.com

E-mail: info@bookleafpub.com

ISBN: 9789395950992

First edition 2022

*To my family, for their steadfast support,
encouragement, and love.*

*To Joy, my well-beloved Chihuahua and
constant companion.*

*To the lost souls who inspired these poems,
may you find peace.*

Once Upon a Lifetime

Her hands ache from rhythmic movements
of pen across paper

her life as she knows it
her purpose as she knows it

can be written and changed in a thousand words
a tragic dialog-

the world needs to know.

Ink splashes up her arms
as she becomes one with the fantasy

of what-ifs
that form her very existence in this hostile place

she sits at her desk
sorting through memories

-and priceless moments

an intricate puzzle
of what she thought would never be.
Once she wanted nothing more than to be alone

in her sadness

before she realized-
the world needed

her to be more than she ever thought she could
be.

Imagine

splashes on my knees-
warm
salty
sentimental
waiting, taking its time to become our lifeline

daring daredevils surfed these seas-
now they come to faded knees
wishing again for that sweet
symphony
of sympathy

drawing attention,
believed
conceived
imagine if we couldn't-
breathe

runes

many hands have held the runes of belief
hoping to be the one
to set the fire alight-

the one
the only one
the perfect one
the precious one
the priceless one

but all have been faced with the same set of
challenges

haters
fighters
liars
crossed swords
and arrows chinked

this is what you signed up for
the heartless words spoken from the heartless
tongue

you learn to swim by drowning first

the well

The well is rather small,
its rope frayed at the edges,
ripping apart in many places.
The stones, covered in a furry coating of moss-
and at the bottom are pennies.
Thousands of tiny copper specks,
each bearing the burden of a wish.
In hope did the weary traveler of life pause to
fulfill a myth,
that the complicated equation of personal lives
~could be solved~
at the lightest splash of such a small thing.
The well is covered in tears
that eventually turned into fears
by those who shed them.

unseen

the last word
of the last sentence
i'll ever write

the last breath
of someone
i never knew

and you took joy in it

watching
unseen
struggles
unfold

maybe i was too little then

to understand

how was laughing at my suffering for the greater
good?
the greater good of who?

me?

you?

or someone else
unseen
unheard
made up by your livid

imagination?

these july days

these lights bursting in the sky
how long before they die?
the enjoyment of a moment cast to a million
this emptiness
dank as it may be
is never cold
as desolate as it may be
is never alone
our minds are never quiet
even in the dead of night
even despite
everything we could ever do to make this all
right

Fairytales

A king
A queen
A prince
A princess
A fairytale ending
To tell for generations,
To tuck the young into their beds with happy
thoughts flooding their minds
To give hope to the lost
Who have seen things
That no one should have to see.

A villain
A victim
A viperous snake
Slithering through the reeds
The goosebumps of the dreaded what-ifs
And irrational fears
That keep you in check
With lashes of past regrets.

The flipping of a coin
The chances
The choices
Rejoice in your freedom

From the singed edges
Of the last pages
Of your perfect fairytale ending.

Legacy

What can they take from you now?

What can they strip from barren bones
and a crushed soul?

Your life perhaps, but never your existence.
On the ground beneath your feet
you'll find the legacy
we wear
on worn faces
and dry lips
and salty wounds-
until you can't feel anything more.

I know they say their side is better
and their whispers are louder than screams
but their voices are louder than me
so that's all that anyone will ever see.

What do I know?
What do I have to show
if my words don't grow?

Will my legacy
be burned into the ground-
not forgotten but never read aloud?

Or maybe for once
the universe will listen to me
even if I speak ever so softly.

hope

hope
hope
hope
a word so fleeting it keeps retreating-
hope
hope
hope
you must keep hoping, groping for something-
hope
hope
hope
spicy and sweet until it reaches out of reach-
hope
hope
hope
do you possibly understand what it's like to be
stranded-
on land
on sand
on an ocean of tears
and years
of fears
hope
hope
hope

hoping every day
for every way
-anything we can say
to make it all okay

Amongst the Trees

15

Before i forget and become a part of the trees
Before i fall on faded knees
Promise the ghost of who i used to be
Always to be free.

Last Words

There's this saying that people say,
when their words run dry.
There's this saying that people say,
to numb this pain.
These words are cherished by those who don't
speak,
their words are weak-
and hollow are their bones
because they've lost all integrity.
There's this saying, the last words are many
"I'm sorry for everything-"
the tongue will tell you its lies.

Written in the Stars

The stars,
They never lie-
The stars,
They always die.
Beauty is a thing
Preserved by time.
Time passes so quickly
But so slowly-
60 seconds to a minute,
60 minutes to an hour,
24 hours to a day,
7 days to a week,
4 weeks to a month,
12 months to a year,
Thousands of years
Are their lifetime
But nothing lasts forever.

Fine

I've written all the letters
and cried all the tears
of five solid years
let my words be crumbled on the doorstep of
your mind
just know
I wouldn't go back in time
to pretend it's fine

a shadow

a shadow of who we once were
for the purpose of what is to come
a tingling, burning fear of change alight
a hope
a dream
the last flickering candle melted
into the palm of your hand
yes
a shadow of who we once were
for the purpose of what is to come

In the Sky

I'll see you in the sky
one day.

I'll see your legacy written in the aligning stars,
yes, one day I'll see you in the sky.

I'll see the comets of your never-ending wishes
pass by.

I'll see your tears like a black hole
in the night.

I'll see you one day, dancing like a shadow
with the dragonflies.

I'll see you in the sky someday
and you'll look like a ghost-

instead of the tinkling of a lonely heart
because that's what you are.

Close Your Eyes

Close your eyes my friend and breathe in the
sweet smell of honey.
Close your eyes my enemy and breathe in the
sweet smell of victory.
Close your eyes my captor and breathe in the
sweet smell of freedom.
Close your eyes my warrior and breathe in the
sweet smell of peace.
Close your eyes my hater and breathe in the
sweet smell of sorrow.
Close your eyes my daydreamer and breathe in
the sweet smell of reality.

Stone-Cold Face

A stone-cold face
Without a trace
Of all that emotion

I crave a way
To say
Okay

To a stone-cold face

who doesn't care   who doesn't stare   who
doesn't speak   whose words are weak

I crave a way
To run away

From
A stone-cold face
But I must return
The deathly glare
That I wear
In the company
Of a stone-cold face.

The Carpenter

The carpenter stands before her work bench-
a bed of wood shavings
surrounding
an intricate structure,

a perfectly carved bird.

Its wings spread out,
Its head tilted
slightly
up to the heavens,
its eyes mirroring the longing for freedom the
carpenter feels herself.

She traces a callused finger across the smooth
surface of the wood-
a smile crosses her lips
as she picks it up,
and one worn foot before the other
places her burdened masterpiece upon the empty
mantle.

The Wielder of the Words

24

He wields the words with powerful intentions.

His voice echoes down cavernous halls,

he wields them like a weapon.

Words, the true controllers of the world:

promises made

hearts broken

suffering left alone-

yet, we worry about he who wields the words.

Why is his voice heard above the rest?

Is it simply because he shouts?

It Comes Through You

It comes through you
not from you,

these words.

Message in a cracked bottle,
lost to the seas of despair,

something hidden

something stolen
from the lifeless hands

of crystal sands.

Loss, inspiration
inspiration, pain.

Hold on

to something
that can't be held-

hold on

until time freezes
and these warm summer days

become something more-

It comes through you
not from you

these words...

A Wisp of Time

I saw you one day
sitting in your yard
in the white lawn chair
you always kept on your porch.

I saw you one day,
your hair a shade of grey
I never thought you would have.

Time takes a toll
on a shadow
of a memory
and I'll never know
what happened next.

I've learned to resign
from the things
I can't control-
like what you do
with your leftovers
of a mangled life

are you proud to have led it?

I'll let you regret it,
as much as you let me
into your house
into your home
into your mind

I'll just be
a wisp of time.

www.ingramcontent.com/pod-product-compliance
Lightning Source LLC
Chambersburg PA
CBHW060926130726

48001CB00006B/2444